OAuth 2.0

Introduction to API Security with OAuth 2.0

Table of Contents

Introduction

OAuth is a very useful standard when it comes to working with client-server applications. They help in improving the functionality of sharing resources between these. This is why you should know how to use this standard. This book will guide you in learning the standard.

Chapter 1- Definition

OAuth means an open standard which is used for the purpose of authorization. The OAuth 2.0 was developed with the intention of improving the simplicity of the client side of applications. It works by providing special flows for authorization for your desktop applications, web applications, mobile phones, and devices for the living room. With this standard, the client applications will find it easy for them to access resources which belong to the server application on the behalf of the owner of the resource. Note that this will be done securely, and in a delegated manner.

This is done by providing a means by which the owners of resources will provide a third-party access to their resources without the need for sharing the necessary credentials. This standard was designed so that it could be used with the HTTP protocol. For the resources to be accessed by the third-party clients, access tokens have to be assigned to these machines by the authorization server. The client machines will then use the access tokens which have been assigned to them for the purpose of accessing the resources which are protected by the resource server. In most cases, the standard is used by internet users for accessing third-party websites by the use of Google, Microsoft, Facebook, and Twitter, and there will be no need for them to expose their websites.

Chapter 2- Roles of OAuth 2.0

The following roles for both users and applications are defined in OAuth 2.0:

Resource Server

Resource Owner

Authorization Server

Client Application

The resource server is the server which is performing the task of hosting the resources. A good example of this is Google or Facebook.

The resource owner is the person or the application which possesses the data which needs to be shared. An example of this is a user who owns a Google or Facebook account. The resource which they possess should be their data. The owner of this resource does not have to be a person, but can also be an application.

The client application in our case will be the application which is performing a request so as to access the resource(s) which has been stored on the resource server. These are the resources which should be owned by the resource owner. An example of a client application is a particular game application which might request access to the Twitter account of someone.

In the case of the authorization server, it should be the server which is performing an authorization to the client application so that it can be able to access the resources of the resource owner.

Note that the resources are stored in the resource server, so this must also be accessed. However, you need to know that both the resource server and the authorization server can be built up into a single server. However, this does not have to be the case.

The reason is that the feature might not be interesting to all of us. In the OAuth 2.0 standard, there is no specification on how communication between these two servers should be done once they have been implemented differently. However, this decision can be seen to be an internal design one which should be made by the authorization server and the resource server developers.

Chapter 3- Types of Clients in OAuth 2.0

In OAuth 2.0, the role of client is divided into types and profiles. This is what we need to discuss in this chapter.

OAuth 2.0 has two types of clients:

Confidential

Public

When the client in your case is public, this will be an indication that it will not be in a position to keep the password as confidential. A good example of this is the desktop application or a mobile phone application which has a client password already embedded in it. If you have this kind of application, then cracking it becomes very easy, and this will mean that the passwords will be revealed. The same case will apply to a Javascript application which is running inside a user's browser. For them to look into the application, the Javascript debugger can be used and the password for the client will observed.

When the client being used is a confidential one, it will be in a position to keep the password as confidential to the world. The authorization server is responsible for assigning this password to the client app. The password will also be tasked with identifying the client app to the authorization server for the purpose of avoiding fraud. A web application is a good example of a confidential client, and in this case, only the administrator will be in a position to access the server and the client password will be visible.

Client profiles

There are client profiles in OAuth 2.0. What they mean is that they are a type of concrete applications which can either be public or confidential. They include the following:

User Agent

Web Application

Native

User Agent Application

This is used for description of a Javascript application which will be executed in the browser. In this case, our browser will act as the user agent. It is possible for us to store a user agent application in the web server, but the app will only run in the user agent once it has been downloaded. A good example of this is a game written in Javascript and one which can only be executed in the browser.

Web Application

This describes an application which is being executed on a web server. A web application is made up of the browser part and the server part. If the application is in need of accessing the resource server, the client app will be in a position to store the password on the server. This will be an indication that the password will be confidential.

Native Application

This is used for description of a mobile phone or a desktop application. For these to be used, they must be installed on a device such as a mobile phone or a tablet or even the user's computer. Once this has been done, the password for the client will be stored on the computer or the device.

Hybrid Applications

With some applications, they are just a hybrid of the profiles discussed above. It is possible for a native application to have a server part, and this will be used for performing a part of the job, such as the process of storing the data. In this version of OAuth standard, this is not talked about. However, what happens is that once this type of application is used, then the authentication process of any of the profiles discussed above is used.

Chapter 4- Authorization in OAuth 2.0

The resources for an application are usually stored on the resource server. Whenever the client needs to access these resources, it has to obtain an "authorization grant." This chapter will show on how to obtain this.

Before your client application requests access for the resources of the resource server, it has to be registered with the application server which is associated with the resource server. The registration is usually done as a one-time task. Once the registration has been completed, it will become and remain valid unless one chooses to revoke the registration of the client app.

It is during this process of registration that the client app will be assigned with a Client ID and a password which is the Client Secret. This is done by the authorization server. Note that the details for the Client ID and the secret for a particular client app will be unique on the associated authorization server. It is also possible for a single client application to perform a registration with multiple and different authorization servers. In this case, each of the authorization servers will have a different Client ID for the client application.

For the client to access or to request access to the resources of the resource server, the process of authentication has to be done. In this case, the client app must specify the client ID and the secret and if found to be correct, the access will be granted. Note that the authentication details are sent to the authorization server.

During the registration process, a URI for redirection should also be provided. This is the URI which is to be used once access to the resource by the resource owner has been granted. After the client app has been successfully authorized by the resource owner via an authorization server, the resource owner will then be redirected to the client app, and then to the redirect URI.

The Authorization Grant

This is given by the resource owner to the client application. Note that this must be done in cooperation with the authorization server which is associated with the resource server.

There are four types of authorization grants which are available in OAuth 2.0. Each exhibits different characteristics when it comes to security.

These include the following:

Resource Owner Password Credentials

Authorization Code

Implicit

Client Credentials

These will be discussed in this chapter.

Implicit

The implicit authorization grant is the same as the authorization code grant. The only exception with this is that the access token is sent to your client application once the user is done with the authorization process. This means that the return of this token is done after the user agent has been redirected to the redirect URI.

This is an indication that the access of the access token will be done in the user agent or in the native application which is taking part in the implicit authorization grant. The storage of the access token in the web server is not done securely.

Once this has been done, the client app will only be able to send its Client ID to the authorization server. In case there was a need for the client app to send out its secret, then this will mean that it will have to be stored in the native application or the user agent. This will make it easy for hackers to access

it.
The process of an implicit authorization grant is always performed or done in the native client application or in the user agent. The user agent or the native application will receive the access token from its authorization server.

Authorization Code

The process of an authorization grant by use of an authorization code works as shown in the steps given below:

The client application is accessed by the resource owner which is the user in our case.

The user is informed by the client application to login into the client app, and this should be done via the authorization server. An example of this is Facebook, Twitter, or Google.

The client application will then redirect the user to the authorization server. This is what usually happens whenever a user tries to login to their client app via the authorization server. The client app will also send its Client ID to the authorization server. This will make it easy for the authorization server to know the client application which is trying to access the resources which it owns.

The user will then perform a login to the system via the authorization server. If the login process succeeds, the server will ask the user to permit the grant of its resources to the client application. If this is accepted, the user will then be redirected to the client application.

Once the redirection to the client app is done, the user will then be redirected by the authorization server to a specific URI. Note that this will be the URI which the authorization server had registered the client app with ahead of time. During the process of redirection, an authorization code will also be sent, and this will act as a representation of the authorization process.

Once the URI for redirection has been accessed, the authorization server and the client application will be directly connected. The client application will then have to send its authorization code together with its Client ID and the Client Secret. These will be sent to the authorization server.

In case the authorization server accepts all of the above mentioned details of the client application, it will send an access token back to the client app. Otherwise, this will not happen.

This access token can then be used by the client application for the purpose of requesting access to the resources of the resource server. This shows that the token issued will be used as a user (resource owner), authentication of the client, and as an authorization for the purpose of accessing the resources.

That is how the process is done.

Resource Owner Password Credentials

This works by granting access to the client application, so that it can be able to access the credentials of the resource owner. This will mean that, for example, a user will be in a position to use the username and the password for their Twitter account in the client application. This will be an indication that the client application will be in a position to use the Twitter credentials, that is, the username and the password so as to access the resources of the Twitter.

For us to use the password credentials for the resource owner, a lot of trust on the part of the client application will be needed. If the application is not trusted at all, then avoid typing your credentials in it. The password credentials for the resource owner will always be used by the native client applications or the user agent client applications.

Client Credentials

This type of authorization is used when the client app is in need of calling functions or accessing the resources of the resource server, and these resources are not related to any user or resource owner. A good example of this is when we have a FourSquare and we need to get a list of venues from it. It is not a must that we deal with a specific FourSquare user.

Chapter 5- Oath 2.0 Endpoints

There are a set of endpoints which are defined in OAuth 2.0. This is just a Uniform Resource Identifier (URI) located on the web server. An example of this is an address of a JSP page, Java servlet, ASP.NET page, or a PHP page.

The following endpoints are defined:

Authorization Endpoint

Token Endpoint

Redirection Endpoint

Both the token endpoint and the authorization endpoint will be located on the authorization server. However, the redirection endpoint will be located on the client application.

In OAuth 2.0, there is no specification on how one can Let us discuss the endpoints mentioned above.

Authorization Endpoint

This is used to represent the endpoint on the authorization server where the resource owner performs the login process. It is after the login process that the client application is granted authorization.

Redirect Endpoint

This represents the endpoint in the client application where we redirect our resource owner to, and this should be after the authorization has been granted to the authorization endpoint.

Chapter 6- Requests and Responses in OAuth 2.0

Once the client application has requested authorization and the access tokens, HTTP requests will be sent to the authorization server, to the token endpoints, and to the authorization. The request and the response to be sent forth and back will be determined by the type of the authorization grant. The grants in this case include the following:

Resource Owner Password Credentials Grant

Implicit Grant

Client Credentials Grant

Authorization Code Grant

These were discussed earlier on in this book, so you can revisit Chapter 4 to read more about them.

Authorization Code Requests and Responses

The authorization code grant is made up of two requests and two responses. These include the following:

An authorization request + response

A token request + response

Authorization Request

This is what we send to the authorization endpoint for the purpose of obtaining an authorization code. The request itself is made up of the following parameters:

response_type- this is required, and it must be set to a code.

client_id- this is also required. It is the client identifier, as it has been specified by the authorization server during the process of registration of the client application.

redirect_uri- this parameter is optional. It is the redirect Uri that the client application registered.

Scope- this parameter is optional. It is used to specify the scope of the request if possible.

State- this parameter is optional, but it is highly recommended that you use it in your request. It refers to the client state which needs to be passed on our Client request URI.

Authorization Response

This has the authorization response which we need for the purpose of obtaining our access token. This response should have the parameters described below:

code- This is required. It represents the authorization code to be used.

state- This is required, if it is present in the request. It is the same value as it was sent by the client in the state parameter if this was the case.

Authorization Error Response

It is possible that an error might occur during the process of authorization. If this is the case, then two situations may happen:

The client may not be recognized or authenticated. In this case, we will have sent a wrong redirect URI in our request. If this is the case, then the authorization server should not redirect our resource owner to our redirect URI. What should happen is that the resource owner should be informed of the occurrence of the error.

The second situation will be that our client will be correctly authenticated, but there will be something which will fail. If this is the case, the following error response will be sent to the client, and it will be included in our redirect URI:

The following are the parameters to be used in this case:

error- this parameter is required. It has to be one of the set of the predefined error codes. View the specification for our codes and what they mean.

error_description- this parameter is optional. It must be written in the human readable UTF-8 encoded text for the description of the error. The parameter is intended to be used by developers rather than by end users.

error_uri- this parameter is optional. It represents a URI which points to a human-readable web page having information describing the error.

state- this parameter is required if it is present in the authorization request. It is the same value as it has been sent in the state parameter in the request.

Token Request

Once the authorization code has been obtained, the client will be in a position to obtain this code for the purpose of obtaining the access token. The access token request has the following parameters:

client_id- this parameter is required. It represents the ID of the client application.

client_secret- this parameter is required. It represents the secret code of the client application.

grant_type- this parameter is also required. It has to be set to the authorization code.

code- this parameter is also required. It represents the authorization code which was received by the authorization server.

redirect_URI- in case the request URI was entered in the authorization request, then this parameter will be a must. They must also be identical.

Token Response

Once the access token request has been issued, its response to it will be a JSON string having the access token and some other information as shown below:

```
{ "access_token" : "...",
"token_type"   : "...",
"expires_in"   : "...",
"refresh_token" : "...",
}
```

The property "access_token" is the access token which was provided by our authorization server. The property "token_type" will be the type of the token which the authorization server provided us with. The property "expires_in" will specify the number of seconds after which our access token will expire. Note that once the access token expires, it will no longer be valid. Note that the process of expiring of these token is optional. The property "refresh_token" represents a fresh token which will be used once the token has reached its expiration time.

Implicit requests and Responses

The implicit grant is made up of a single request and a single response.

Implicit Grant Request

This is made up of the following parameters:

response_type- this parameter is required. It must be set to a token.

client_id- this parameter is also required. It is the ID of the client as it was assigned by the authorization server during the process of registration of the client.

redirect_URI- this parameter is optional. It represents the redirect URI which was assigned by client application.

scope- this parameter is optional. It represents the possible scope which can be taken by the request.

State- although this is an optional parameter, it is highly recommended that you specify it. It represents any of the client states which needs to be passed to the URI for the client request.

Implicit Grant Response

This type of response is made up of the following parameters:

access_token- this parameter is required. It represents the access token which was granted by the authorization server.

token_type- this parameter must be provided. It represents the type of token which is to be used.

expires_in- this is a recommended parameter. It represents the number of seconds after which the access token will expire.

Scope- this parameter is optional. It represents the type of scope taken by the access token.

State- this parameter must be specified if it was used in the authorization request. Its value in this case has to be the same as the state parameter of the request.

Chapter 7- Grant Request/Response for Resource Owner Password Credentials

The credentials authorization for the resource owner password is made up of a single request and a single response.

The password credentials grant request for the resource owner is made up of the following parameters:

grant_type- this parameter is required. It has to be set to the password.

Username- this parameter is required. It specifies the username of the resource owner. It has to be uTF-8 encoded.

Password-this parameter has to be specified. It specifies the password of the resource owner, and it has to be UTF-encoded.

Scope- this is an optional parameter, and it specifies the scope of the authorization process.

In the case of the grant response, it will be a JSON structure which has the access token. It takes the following structure:

```
{ "access_token" : "...",
"token_type"   : "...",
"expires_in"   : "...",
"refresh_token" : "...",
}
```

The property"access_token" specifies the name of the access token which was assigned by the authorization server. The "token_type" specifies the type of token which authorization server created. The "expires_in" property will specify the number of seconds after which the access token will expire. Note that once the token has expired, it will be no longer valid. Note that it is optional for the token expire. The property "refresh_token" represents the refresh token which will be used in case of the expiration of the access token. It will be used for the purpose of obtaining a new access token in case the one which is returned in the response is invalid.

Chapter 8- Using Doorkeeper to protect Grape API

The OAuth 2.0 protocol can be used for the protection of the Grape Application Program Interface (API). The development of this API was done in Grape, and then mounted under the Ruby on Rails.

For the protection to be done, the following things have to be built:

Resource owner- the role who is to take on the task of granting authorization to the third-party apps. This is the user.

Authorization server- this will represent all of the details of the authorization server. These include the following:

Clients- a basic Create, Read, Update, and Delete (CRUD) interface will be needed for the purpose of managing the client applications.

Access token- a model for the purpose of storing the access tokens is needed.

Authorization Endpoint- this is for the purpose of processing the Auth Code grant or the implicit grant flows.

Token Endpoint- this is where the access tokens are processed.

Resource server- this is the location to be accessed by the applications, which is the API. Some of the APIs which one has to have an access token for the purpose of accessing them are known as "protected resources."

The implementation of most components is done via solutions which are in existence. These are given below:

Authorization Server (OAuth 2 Provider) - Doorkeeper

Resource Server (API) - Grape

Resource Owner (the User) - Devise

Guard - Manually integrated Rack::OAuth2 into Grape.

The property "doorkeeper_for" can only be used on Ruby on Rails. It can also be used with Rack. Note that this standard is just a Rack middleware. This is an indication that these have to be manually mashed up.

The following are the necessary steps for protection of the API:

Step 1- Building the Resource Owner Business Logic

This will be built with devise just as we have mentioned. This is easy to understand, and especially for those who are Ruby experts. This is why we will not explore this.

Step 2: Building the API (the Resource Server)

In this step, we will use Grape so as to develop the API. The reason for this is that there is no need for the request to pass through numerous stacks on the Rails.

Step 3: Building the Provider (the Authorization Server)

In this step, we will use the DoorKeeper, since this is based on Rails.
Begin by performing an installation of the DoorKeeper Gem. To do this, just execute the following command:

gem 'doorkeeper'

The command "bundle install" should also be executed. The following sequence of commands needs to be executed for the purpose of installation:

```
$ rails generate doorkeeper:install
$ rails generate doorkeeper:migration
$ rake db:migrate
```

The next step should be changing our configuration file so that the DoorKeeper is made to authenticate the Resource Owner by use of the devise.

The file is "config/initializers/doorkeeper.rb," and it should be edited to the following:

Authenticating the Resource Owner with Devise
resource_owner_authenticator do
current_user || warden.authenticate!(:scope => :user)
end

That is what we can do. Our authorization server is now ready. The following are the tables created by the DoorKeeper:

oauth_applications- this is the registry for our clients.

oauth_access_grants- this is the registry for our Auth codes. These are issued in our first step of Grant type flow for the authorization code.

oauth_access_tokens- this is used for storing the access tokens which we issued, and this includes the refresh tokens which correspond to this, and they have been disabled by default.

The following routes are registered by the DoorKeeper:

new- the path for this method is "/oauth/authorize."

create- the path for this is "/oauth/authorize." It is used for specifying the action taken once the user has granted an authorization request.

destroy- the path for this is "/oauth/authorize." It is used for specification of the action once the user has denied the authorization request.

show- this has the path "/oauth/authorize/:code." It is used for local testing purposes.

update- the path for this is "/oauth/authorize." Used for the purpose of Unknown Update Grant.

resources- this has the path "/oauth/applications." It is used for the purpose of managing the clients.

index- this takes the path "/oauth/authorized_applications." It specifies the resource owner for the purpose of management of the authorized clients.

destroy-   this   takes   the   path "/oauth/authorized_applications/:id." The Resource Owner is tasked with the responsibility of managing the clients.

When the action for show for the Authorization Endpoint has been used, only the grant code will be displayed, and this can be used for the purpose of local testing. There is no actual method in the update actions for the purpose of catching this. This might or might not be a dead feature. Some of its possibilities are:

It provides a Token Endpoint and Authorization Endpoint.

It provides the Token Debug Endpoint, of which this can be used in verification of the Token in Implicit Flow.

It might come with a management interface for clients.

It might also provide an interface to the users for the purpose of managing the authorized clients.

Note that with the DoorKeeper, everything which is needed by the authorization server is readily provided.

Step 4- Creation of a Client for testing purpose

Once the authorization server has been built, a new client can then be created.

For this to be done, one should start by opening the "/oauth/applications/new." In the field for Redirect URI, fill in "http://localhost:12345/auth/demo/callback" and then submit what you have done. Note that it is not a must for you to have a web server at your localhost:12345. The token or the grant code can be grabbed for the purpose of testing.

Step 5- Obtaining the Access Token

At this point, we can try to obtain or get our access token. The client should be simulated so that it can execute the Authorization Code Grant Flow, and this is what we are going to do. This should be done as follows:

Begin by opening the show page for the client which we just created. A page which displays the application ID, the secret, and other information specific to the client will be displayed on the page. An Authorize link will also be displayed at the bottom of this page. Just click on the above link, and the following will be opened:

http://localhost:9999/oauth/authorize
?client_id=4a407c6a8d3c75e17a5560d0d0e4507c77b047940
db6df882c86aaeac2c788d6
&redirect_uri=http%3A%2F%2Flocalhost%3A12345%2Fauth
%2Fdemo%2Fcallback
&response_type=code

You can have additional lines for the purpose of increasing the readability. What happens is that the client will send a request to the Authorization Endpoint, this will be for the Grant Code, and will present the Client ID or the Redirect URI. The Doorkeeper will then ask you whether to authorize or deny (the Resource Owner). In this case, Authorize will be selected.

The next location to be taken to will not be opened by the browser, and this should be the Redirect URI which was specified during the creation of the app.

At this point, the client should have the grant code. It should then perform an exchange of the grant code for the purpose of Access Token via the back channel to the Authorization Server.

Step 6- Building the Guard on the Authorization Server

If Grape was used for building the API, then there will be no Guard solution which can be used. For those who used Rails to create the API, then note that "doorkeeper_for" has not been implemented fully currently. However, there is a solution to this. You just have to take a Bearer Token middleware which belongs to Rack, which is OAuth 2.0, and then attach it to the Grape. Some login for "ddorkeeper_for" should also be used. That is how it can simply be done. If you follow the steps carefully, then the outcome will be good.

Step 7- Installation of Rack Middleware for Fetching of Access Token

A block which OAuth 2.0 will call the middleware has to be provided when we are installing the Rack. However, for this to be called, the request must come with an OAuth 2.0 token, that is:

If the request has the "Authorization: Bearer XXX" header or the query parameter "?access_token=xxx," the block will be called.

In case the request lacks the parameters mentioned above, then the block will not be called. In this case, this will be passed to the next stack in the middleware.

What happens with this middleware is that it only stores the return value of a call on a particular block, and this is stored in the "request.env["some key"]." This is an indication that this one is used for the purpose of fetching the access token, but not checking on the validity of the access token and then completing the request. The process of checking for the validity of the Access Token is done at the API layer.

What we do is that we install the middleware, and then use it for the purpose of fetching the Access Token for the string. This is shown below:

```
included do
    # OAuth2 Resource Server Authentication
    use Rack::OAuth2::Server::Resource::Bearer, ' API Name '
do |request|
        # The authenticator will only fetch the raw token string
```

```
      # It must produce the access token to store it in the env
      request.access_token
    end
end
```

Step 8- Making a Private Method take out the Access Token which has been fetched

This is the string. As we had said, the storage of the token by the middleware is done in "request.env." To be actual, this is the   location "request.env[Rack::OAuth2::Server::Resource::ACCESS_TOK EN]." Once we have taken it out, we will get the following:

```
helpers do
   private
   def get_token_string
     # The storage of the token was done after the authenticator
was invoked.
     # This can be nil. In this case, the authenticator will not
check its existence.

request.env[Rack::OAuth2::Server::Resource::ACCESS_TOKE
N]
   end
  end
```

Step 9- Making a Private method convert a Token String to an Instance

A token string is just a string, and the actual instance of the access token has to be found in the model. The logic can be found in the helper "doorkeeper_for." It is after this that you notice the "AccessToken.authenticate" can be directly invoked. Once the above has been invoked, if an instance is found, it will be returned, if not, then this will return nil. This is shown below:

```
helpers do
  private
  def find_access_token(token_string)
    Doorkeeper::AccessToken.authenticate(token_string)
  end
 end
```

Step 10- Making a service verify the Access Token

This is a service built as a module named "OAuth2::AccessTokenValidationService." In my case, I have stored it in "app/services." Its work is validation of the token in terms of not expired, has sufficient scopes and is not revoked. To validate the parameters "expired" and "revoked," we use the "Doorkeeper::AccessToken's" which are in-built methods. The sufficiency of scopes is used for the purpose of validation of whether the authorized scopes which we have used are equal to or more than the scopes which are required for our case. Once this has been done, our validator will give us one of the four constants which you have defined in the module, and these include EXPIRED, VALID, REVOKED, and INSUFFICIENT_SCOPE.

What I do is that I use the helper "validate_access_token" in the Grape Endpoint, and this will enhance the ease of access, meaning that the result of the validation process will be returned directly. These are the four results which we have mentioned above. It is after this that the caller will determine how it will respond, and this will be determined by the result from the validation process.

This is shown below:

```
helpers do
  private
  def validate_access_token(access_token, scopes)

OAuth2::AccessTokenValidationService.validate(access_token
, scopes: scopes)
  end
end
```

The process of "set comparison" is the most effective way that we can compare scope sufficiency. If we find that the set of the authorized scope is a superset of the set of required scopes, then the scope is said to be sufficient. If you find otherwise, then the scope will be termed to be insufficient. However, for those who would like to implement a particular logic such as "Scope X includes Scope Y," an algorithm has to be used.

The following shows a simple set of algorithms for the purpose of comparison:

If there are no scopes required, any Access Token will have sufficient scopes. Return True.

If required scopes are found, compare the set of two scopes, and then determine whether the set of the scopes which are authorized is a superset of the scopes which are required.

In Ruby, there is an inbuilt data structure which can be used for the purpose of conversion of an array into a set. This is shown below:

```
protected
def sufficent_scope?(token, scopes)
  if scopes.blank?
    # if we have no any scopes required, the scopes of token will
be sufficient.
    return true
  else
    # If we have scopes required, then check whether
    # the authorized scopes set is a superset of the required
scopes set
    required_scopes = Set.new(scopes)
```

```
  authorized_scopes = Set.new(token.scopes)
  return authorized_scopes >= required_scopes
end
end
```

That is the code for doing that.

Step 11- Making the Guard deny a Request with no valid Access Token

We should now define our method which will be used for the purpose of denying API uses.

For us to make the program flow in a clearer way, we should define an exception for each error which will be caught.
  In Grape, errors can be handled by "rescue_from," or we can just raise the built in exceptions for "Rack::OAuth2" directly in the exceptions.

The logic for doing this should flow as follows:

Begin by fetching the token string.

If we have been given no token, then this will be an indication that our client will not be aware that there is a need for it to present a token. We wil then raise the "MissingTokenError" exception.

The status of the response should be 401 according to spec. This should not have a detailed message for the error.

If a token is available and it has been found in the database, the exception "MissingTokenError" should be raised.

Our response is expected to have the status of 401 according to the spec. The associate error should be the "Invalid Token Error."

If we find our token in the database, we should perform a verification to check on whether this can be used for accessing the API. You should also check on whether it has expired or it has been revoked. If there are required scopes, the authorized scopes should be checked as follows:

If the obtained result is VALID, the "@current_user" should be assigned to the user or the Resource Owner, which is bound to the Access Token.

Otherwise, respective exceptions should be raised.

In case our validation fails due to insufficient scopes, our status for the response should be 403 with the message "Insufficient Scope Error." Otherwise, it should have the status of 401 and the error "Invalid Token Error" according to the spec.

This is shown in the code given below:

```
helpers do
def guard!(scopes: [])
t_string = get_token_string()
if t_string.blank?
raise MissingTokenError
elsif (access_token = find_access_token(t_string)).nil?
raise TokenNotFoundError
else
case validate_access_token(access_token, scopes)
when
Oauth2::AccessTokenValidationService::INSUFFICIENT_SC
OPE
raise InsufficientScopeError.new(sc)
when Oauth2::AccessTokenValidationService::EXPIRED
```

```
      raise ExpiredError
    when Oauth2::AccessTokenValidationService::REVOKED
      raise RevokedError
    when Oauth2::AccessTokenValidationService::VALID
      @current_user = User.find(access_token.resource_owner_id)
    end
  end
end
end
```

Step 12- Forwarding Exceptions to Exceptions which are rack Built-in Rack::OAuth2

To implement this, we have to use the "rescue_from" in Grape, and this will catch all of the exceptions. This can also be raised directly.

However, you need to note that there are "error_description" strings in the "Bearer::ErrorMethods." There is a description string for each of the error codes.

However, once exceptions have been raised directly from the Rack authenticator, these will be automatically filled-up.

In case error responder middlewares are called, these will not be filled up directly. This will mean that the filling up of these will have to be done manually.

In case the resulting error is due to the fact that we have not presented a token, then it will be easy for us to assume that our client does not know whether it is needed to perform the validation.

This will mean that we will not have to use any of the "error" defined in the spec.

In this case, the property "error_description" can also be omitted.

The response in this case should be Bearer::Unauthorized middleware having middleware.

If the error resulted due to the fact that token was not found, revoked, or even expired, "invalid_token" should be used for the error code.

In this case, the same "error_description" can be used.

The same description for the error can be used in the implementation, and the requirements of the spec will still be fulfilled.

The response in this case will be 401 with the Bearer::Unauthorized middleware.

If the resultant error was as a result of insufficient scope of the token scope, the error code to be used should be "insufficient_scope."

The response in this case should be 403 with Bearer::Forbiddden middleware.

The implementation of Rack::OAuth2 fails to respond with the WWW-Authenticate header. This is only required in the 401 response.

All the error messages with the inclusion of "scope" will be found in the response body for JSON.

A fork which fills error messages in the header for WWW-Authenticate has been implemented.

In this implementation, we have not cared about the "realm" and the "error_uri." In this case, the realm will fall back to the Rack::OAuth2's default one.

The code for this is given below:

```ruby
included do |base|
install_error_responders(bs)
end
# ...
module ClassMethods
private
def install_error_responders(bs)
err_classes = [ MissingTokenError, TokenNotFoundError,
ExpiredError, RevokedError, InsufficientScopeError]
base.send              :rescue_from,          *err_classes,
oauth2_bearer_token_error_handler
end
def oauth2_bearer_token_error_handler
Proc.new {|e|
resp = case e
when MissingTokenError
Rack::OAuth2::Server::Resource::Bearer::Unauthorized.new
when TokenNotFoundError
Rack::OAuth2::Server::Resource::Bearer::Unauthorized.new(
:invalid_token,
"Bad Token Accessed.")
end
response.finish
}
end
end
```

That is how the implementation can be done.

Step 13- implementing a Guard on our API

The copying of the usage has been done from the "doorkeeper_for :all." This is used in "require OAuth 2 Token for the endpoints under the API." For Grape users, this has to be implemented as a class method in our class "Grape::API." This is why I have put this in the module named "ClassMethods." This can be called in Grape::API, and a filter for "before" will be inserted, and all of the endpoints which we have will have to go through the filter. This is shown in the code given below:

```
module ClassMethods
def guard_all!(scopes: [])
before do
guard! scopes: scopes
end
end
end
```

That is how simply it can be implemented.

Step 14- Locking Up the API with OAuth2

When OAuth 2 is required on a single Endpoint, then this can be done as follows:

```
module M1
  class MyAPI < Base
    get "secret" do
      guard! # A valid OAuth 2 Access Token I required to use this Endpoint
      { :secret => "You can only see this if you are an expert. ;)" }
    end
  end
end
```

When the OAuth2 is required at all the endpoints under the API, this can be done as follows:

```
module M1
  class MyAPI < Base
    guard_all!  # A valid OAuth 2 Access Token is required to use all Endpoints

    get "secret1" do
      { :secret_a => "Hello, #{current_user.email}" }
    end
    get "secret_b
_b" do
      { :secret_b => "You can only see this if you are an expert ;)"
}
    end
  end
end
```

If you send a request which has no valid token, then this will be rejected as shown below:

```
$ curl -i http://localhost:9999/api/m1/secret/secret1.json
HTTP/1.1 401 Unauthorized
WWW-Authenticate: Bearer realm="The API"
Content-Type: application/json
Cache-Control: no-cache
{"error":"unauthorized"}
```

If a valid token is passed, this will be passed, and the user of the token will be shown. This is shown below:

```
$ curl -i http://localhost:9999/api/m1/secret/secret_a.json \
> -H "Authorization: Bearer
a14gh674309df32fbb6a3bgc6cba25f32a28bdf931a74ead06ca9
04dc5281b4c"
HTTP/1.1 200 OK
Content-Type: application/json
Cache-Control: max-age=0, private, must-revalidate
{"secret_a":"Hello, name@gmail.com"}
```

It is recommended that once you have made any changes you restart your Rails server. Don't forget to do this.

However, after opening the link for "Authorize," you will not see the URL which has the URL parameter. This to be first manipulated manually. The parameter "scope=top_secret" has to be added as shown below:

http://localhost:9999/oauth/authorize

```
?client_id=
a14gh674309df32fbb6a3bgc6cba25f32a28bdf931a74ead06ca9
04dc5281b4c
&redirect_uri=http%3A%2F%2Flocalhost%3A12345%2Fauth
%2Fdemo%2Fcallback
&response_type=code
&scope=top_secret
```

After that, you will be asked to either deny or authorize again. This will mean that the authorization server will understand whether the client had been granted with some specific scopes in the past. Once the process of authorization is completed, another grant code will be sent to the client. It will then be possible for this to be exchanged with the Access Token.

2 Endpoints can now be added to MyAPI and these are required to have some specific scopes:


```
get "top_secret" do
guard! scopes: [:top_secret]
{ :top_secret => "ToP S4CG37 :p" }
end
get "choice_of_sg" do
guard! scopes: [:el, :psy, :congroo]
{ :says => "El. Psy. Congroo." }
End
```


If the endpoint "top_secret" is accessed with the previous Access Token, this will be rejected:


```
$ curl -i
http://localhost:9999/api/m1/sample/top_secret.json \
```

```
> -H "Authorization: Bearer
a14gh674309df32fbb6a3bgc6cba25f32a28bdf931a74ead06ca9
04dc5281b4c "
HTTP/1.1 403 Forbidden
Content-Type: application/json
Cache-Control: no-cache
{
"error":"insufficient_scope",
"error_description":"Request will require higher privileges
than ones provided by the access token.",
"scope":"top_secret"
}
```

If the endpoint "top_secret" is accessed with our previous Access Token, then it will reject as shown below:

```
$ curl -i
http://localhost:9999/api/m1/sample/top_secret.json \
> -H "Authorization: Bearer
a14gh674309df32fbb6a3bgc6cba25f32a28bdf931a74ead06ca9
04dc5281b4c "
HTTP/1.1 403 Forbidden
Content-Type: application/json
Cache-Control: no-cache
{
"error":"insufficient_scope",
"error_description":"The request will require higher privileges
than the ones provided by the access token.",
"scope":"top_secret"
}
```

In case a new token is used, then we will pass this.

Conclusion

It can be concluded that OAuth2 is a standard which is open, and it is used for the purpose of authorization. The standard was developed so that it can enhance the ease with which the client side of applications is developed. The standard just provides your web application, desktop application, or even a mobile application with specific flows for the purpose of authorization.

When the clients use it, they can securely access the resources of the resource owner on behalf of the resource owner, and the process will be carried out in a much delegated manner. At the same time, resource owners make it easy for third party applications to access their resources and in this case, the resource owner does not have to share its credentials for this to happen.

It just issues the client machines with access tokens which the clients will use for the purpose of accessing the resources of the resource owner. Note that the resources in this case are protected by the resource server, and the issuing of the access tokens is done by the authorization server. In most cases, this standard is used by Internet users for the purpose of accessing third-party websites and they will use Google, Microsoft, and others for this purpose. This book helps you to learn how to use the protocol